For Mila, Ruby, and Gabby

Special thanks to Ranke de Vries for painting the artwork for Fancy Goat.

This book was made possible with generous support from Arts Nova Scotia.

ISBN 978-0-9958692-1-9

Published by Outside the Lines Press
Antigonish, Nova Scotia
www.outsidethelinespress.com

Printed in China

10 9 8 7 6 5 4 3 2 1

For retail and wholesale purchases of **Fancy Goat**, contact the publisher via the above website.

Fancy Goat

by Jeremy Holmes and Justin Gregg

 Outside the Lines Press

My goat was born *Fancy*.

He has his own chauffeur.

He even has a masseuse.

My goat doesn't eat grass.

He prefers éclairs.

He sleeps in a *Fancy* bed.

He has a taste for fine art.

He has an eye for fashion.

My goat is so *Fancy*.
It's out of control.

I'm always polishing his monocle.

And ironing his cravats.

And shining his cufflinks.

And dusting his top hat.

Or is it just my goat?

And he can fly a plane.

Like put away the laundry.

Or help me with the dishes.

Even my DOG can do that.

He is just so un-baaaa-lievably *Fancy*!

Cuteness = 10

Huggability = 10

Elegance = 10

Vanity = 10

Resplendency = 10

Ear length = 10

FANCINESS SCALE

I think I have the fanciest goat in the whole wide world.

My goat might even be the fanciest ANIMAL in the whole wide world!

But if you think my goat is *Fancy*...